The Contemporary Bible Series

JOSHUA
and the Promised Land

Contemporary Bible Serie

JOSHUA and the Promised Lan

Published by Scandinavia Publishing House 201(
Drejervej 15,3   DK-2400 Copenhagen NV, Denmar
Tel. (45) 3531 0330 Fax (45) 3536 033
E-mail: info@scanpublishing.d
Web: www.scanpublishing.d

Text copyright © Contemporary English Versior
Illustrations copyright © Gustavo Maza
Design by Ben Ale
Printed in China
ISBN 978 87 7247 424

JOSHUA
and the Promised Land
Contemporary English Version

Contents

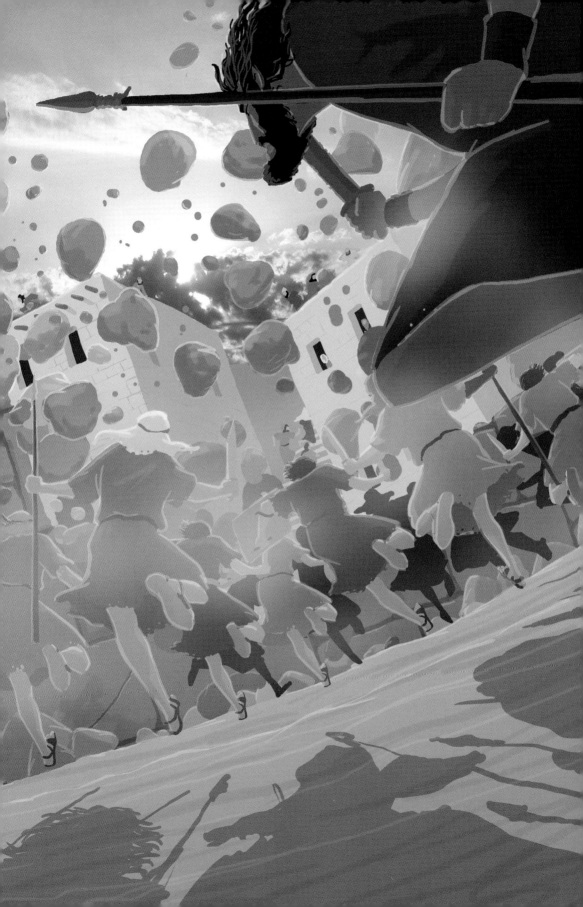

The Second
Ten Commandments

Exodus 34:1-9

One day the Lord said to Moses, "Cut two flat stones like the first ones I made. I will write on them the same commandments that were on the two you broke.

Come up Mount Sinai and meet me at the top."

So Moses cut two flat stones like the first ones, and early the next morning he carried them to the top of Mount Sinai. The Lord God came down in a cloud and stood beside Moses there on the

mountain. Then God passed in front of Moses and called out, "I am the Lord God. I am merciful and very patient with my people. I show great love, and I can be trusted. I keep my promises to my people forever, but I also punish anyone who sins."

Moses quickly bowed down to the ground and worshiped the Lord. He prayed, "Lord, if you really are pleased with me, I pray that you will go with us. It is true that these people are sinful and rebellious, but forgive our sin and let us be your people."

The People Grumble About Being Hungry

Numbers 11:4-15

One day some foreigners among the Israelites became greedy for food. Even the Israelites themselves began moaning, "We don't have any meat! In Egypt we could eat all the fish we wanted, and there were cucumbers, melons, onions, and garlic. But we're starving out here. The only food we have is this manna."

The manna appeared at night with the dew. In the morning the people would collect the manna, grind or crush it into flour, then boil it and make it into thin wafers.

The Israelites stood around their tents complaining. Moses heard them and was upset that they had made the Lord angry. He prayed, "God, I am your servant, so why are you doing this to me? What have I done to deserve this? You've made me responsible for all these people, but they're not my children. They keep whining for meat, but where can I get meat for them? This job is too much for me. How can I take care of all these people by myself? If this is the way you're going to treat me, just kill me now and end my miserable life!"

The Lord Sends Quails

Numbers 11:31-35

Some time later the Lord sent a strong wind that blew quails in from the sea until Israel's camp was completely surrounded with birds. They were piled up about three feet high for miles in every direction. The people picked up quails for two days. Each person filled at least fifty bushels. Then they spread them out to dry. But before the meat could be eaten, the Lord became angry. He sent a disease through the camp.

They buried the people who had been so greedy for meat. They called the place "Graves for the Greedy." Israel then broke camp and traveled to Hazeroth.

Miriam and Aaron Are Jealous of Moses

Numbers 12:1-15

Although Moses was the most humble person in the world, Miriam and Aaron started complaining. They said, "Who does Moses think he is? The Lord has spoken to us, not just to him."

The Lord heard their complaint. He told Moses, Aaron, and Miriam to come to the sacred tent. There the Lord appeared in a cloud. He told Aaron and Miriam to come closer. Then he said, "I, the Lord, speak to prophets in visions and dreams. But my servant Moses is the leader of my people. He sees me face to face, and everything I say to him is perfectly clear. You have no right to criticize my servant Moses."

The Lord became angry at Aaron and Miriam. And after the Lord left and the cloud disappeared from over the sacred tent, Miriam's skin turned white with leprosy.

When Aaron saw what had happened to her, he said to Moses, "Sir, please don't punish us for doing such a foolish thing. Don't let Miriam's flesh rot away like a child born dead!"

So Moses prayed, "Lord God, please heal her."

But the Lord replied, "Make her stay outside the camp for seven days, before coming back." The people of Israel did not move their camp until Miriam returned seven days later.

Twelve Men Are Sent into Canaan

Numbers 13:1-24

The Lord said to Moses, "Choose a leader from each tribe and send them into Canaan to explore the land I am giving you."

Before Moses sent the twelve leaders into Canaan, he said to them, "Find out what those regions are like. Be sure to remember how many people live there, how strong they are, and if they live in open towns or walled cities. See if the land is good for growing crops and find out what kinds of trees grow there. It's time for grapes to ripen, so try to bring back some fruit."

The twelve men left to explore Canaan from the Zin Desert in the south all the way to the town of Rehob in the north. As they went through the Southern Desert, they came to the town of Hebron. In Hebron, they saw the three Anakim clans of Ahiman, Sheshai, and Talmai. When they got to Bunch Valley, they cut off a branch with such a huge bunch of grapes, that it took two men to carry it on a pole. That's why the place was called Bunch Valley. They also took back pomegranates and figs.

The Twelve Scouts Return

Numbers 13:25-33

After forty days of exploring the land of Canaan, the twelve men returned back to camp. "Canaan is an amazing land," they told the people. "Just look at the size of this fruit!" The men passed around the grapes they had brought with them. "But the people there are strong, and the cities have high walls all around them. There are tribes living along the sea, and down in the valleys and all over the desert."

The people began to worry. "How can we capture this land?" they asked each other. "There are too many people living there already." But Caleb wasn't worried. He was one of the Israeli leaders. "Let's take the land," he said. "I know we can do it!"

"There is no way we can take the land," the twelve men told him. "We saw the people there, and they are like giants. They were so big that we felt as little as grasshoppers."

14

Moses Speaks to Israel

Deuteronomy 8:1-18

Moses said to the people of Israel, "Don't forget how the Lord your God has led you through the desert for the past forty years. He wanted to find out if you were truly willing to obey him, so he made you go hungry. Then he gave you manna, a kind of food that you and your ancestors had never even heard about. Over the past forty years, your clothing hasn't worn out, and your feet haven't swollen. Obey the commands the Lord has given you and worship him. The Lord is bringing you into a good land with streams that flow from springs in the

valleys and hills. You won't go hungry. Wheat and barley fields are everywhere. There are vineyards and orchards full of fig, pomegranate, and olive trees, and there is plenty of honey. After you eat and are full, give praise to the Lord. Don't be proud. Don't forget that you were once slaves in Egypt. When you become successful, don't say, 'I'm rich, and I've earned it all myself.' Instead, remember that the Lord your God gives you the strength to make a living. That's how he keeps the promise he made to your ancestors."

17

The Last Days of Moses

Deuteronomy 34:1-10

Sometime later, Moses left the lowlands of Moab. The Lord said, "Moses, this is the land I was talking about when I promised Abraham, Isaac, and Jacob that I would give land to their descendants. I have let you see it, but you will not cross the Jordan and go in."

And so, Moses the Lord's servant died there in Moab, just as the Lord had said. The Lord buried him in a valley near the town of Beth-Peor, but even today no one knows exactly where. Moses was a hundred twenty years old when he died, yet his eyesight was still good, and his body was strong.

The people of Israel stayed in the lowlands of Moab. There they mourned and grieved thirty days for Moses. There has never again been a prophet in Israel like Moses. The Lord spoke face to face with him.

Joshua Becomes the Leader of Israel

Joshua 1:1-9

The Lord spoke to Joshua, who had been the assistant of Moses. The Lord said to him, "My servant Moses is dead. Now you must lead Israel across the Jordan River into the land I'm giving to all of you. Wherever you go, I'll give you that land, as I promised Moses. Joshua, I will always be with you and help you as I helped Moses. No one will ever be able to defeat you."

Then the Lord said, "Long ago I promised the ancestors of Israel that I would give this land to their descendants. So be strong and brave! Be careful to do everything my servant Moses taught you. Never stop reading The Book of the Law he gave you. Day and night you must think about what it says. If you obey it completely, Israel will be able to take this land. I've commanded you to be strong and brave. Don't ever be afraid or discouraged! I am the Lord your God. I will be there to help you wherever you go."

Rahab Helps the Spies

Joshua 2:1-7

Joshua chose two men as spies. He sent them from their camp at Acacia with these instructions: "Go across the river and find out as much as you can about the whole region, especially about the town of Jericho."

The two spies left the Israelite camp and went to Jericho, where they decided to spend the night at the house of a woman named Rahab. But someone found out about them. They told the king of Jericho, "Some Israelite men came here tonight, and they are spies." So the king sent soldiers to Rahab's house to arrest the spies.

Meanwhile, Rahab had taken the men up to the flat roof of her house and had hidden them under some piles of flax plants that she had put there to dry. The soldiers came to her door and demanded, "Let us have the men who are staying at your house. They are spies."

She answered, "Some men did come to my house, but I didn't know where they had come from. They left about sunset, just before it was time to close the town gate. I don't know where they were going. If you hurry, maybe you can catch them." The guards at the town gate let the soldiers leave Jericho. Then the soldiers headed toward the Jordan River to look for the spies at the place where people cross the river.

23

The Eastern Tribes Promise to Help

Joshua 1: 10-15

Joshua ordered the tribal leaders to go through the camp and tell everyone, "In a few days we will cross the Jordan River to take the land that the Lord our God is giving us. Fix as much food as you'll need for the march into the land."

Then Joshua told the men of the tribes of Reuben, Gad, and East Manasseh, "The Lord's servant Moses said that the Lord our God has given you land here on the east side of the Jordan River, where you could live in peace. Your wives and children and your animals can stay here. But all of you that can serve in our army must pick up your weapons and lead the men of the other tribes across the Jordan River. They are your relatives, so you must help them conquer the land that the Lord is giving them. The Lord will give peace to them as he has given peace to you. Then you can come back and settle here in the land that Moses promised you."

Rahab Asks a Favor

Joshua 2:8-14

Back in Jericho, Rahab went back up to her roof. The spies were still awake, so she told them, "I know that the Lord has given Israel this land. Everyone shakes with fear because of you. We heard how the Lord dried up the Red Sea so you could leave Egypt. And we heard how you destroyed those two Amorite kings east of the Jordan River. We know that the Lord your God rules heaven and earth, and we've lost our courage and our will to fight. Please promise me in the Lord's name that you will be as kind to my family as I have been to you."

"Rahab," the spies answered, "If you keep quiet about what we're doing, we promise to be kind to you when the Lord gives us this land. We pray that the Lord will kill us if we don't keep our promise!"

27

The Spies Escape

Joshua 2:15-24

Rahab's house was built into the town wall, and one of her windows faced outside the wall. She gave the spies a rope, showed them the window, and said, "Use this rope to let yourselves down to the ground outside the wall. Then hide in the hills. The men who are looking for you won't be able to find you there. They'll give up and come back after a few days. Then you can be on your way."

The spies said, "You made us promise to let you and your family live. We will keep our promise, but you can't tell anyone why we were here. You must tie this red rope on your window when we attack.

Everyone else in your family must be here with you. But anyone who leaves your house will be killed."

"I'll do exactly what you said," Rahab promised. Then she sent them on their way and tied the red rope to the window.

The spies hid in the hills for three days while the king's soldiers looked for them along the roads. As soon as the soldiers gave up and returned to Jericho, the two spies went down into the Jordan valley and crossed the river. They reported to Joshua and told him everything that had happened. "We're sure the Lord has given us the whole country," they said. "The people there shake with fear every time they think of us."

The Sacred Chest Leads the Way

Joshua 3:1-8

Early the next morning, Joshua and the Israelites packed up and left. They went to the Jordan River and camped there that night. Two days later their leaders went through the camp shouting, "When you see some of the priests carrying the sacred chest, you'll know it is time to cross to the other side. You won't know the way unless you follow the chest. But don't get too close! Stay about half a mile back."

Joshua told the people, "The Lord is going to do some amazing things for us." Then Joshua turned to the priests and said, "Take the chest and cross the Jordan River ahead of us." So the priests picked up the chest by its carrying poles and went on ahead.

The Lord told Joshua, "Beginning today I will show the people that you are their leader. They will know that I am helping you as I helped Moses. Now, tell the priests who are carrying the chest to go a little way into the river and stand there."

Israel Crosses the Jordan River

Joshua 3:9-17, Joshua 4:10-18

Joshua spoke to the people, "Come here and listen to what the Lord our God said he will do! The enemy tribes control the land on the other side of the river. But the living God will be with you when you attack. God is going to prove that he's powerful enough to force them out. Just watch the sacred chest that belongs to the Lord. As soon as the priests carrying the chest step into the Jordan, the water will stop flowing and pile up. It will be as if someone had built a dam across the river. The Lord has also said that each of the twelve tribes should choose one man to represent it."

The priests carrying the chest walked in front, until they came to the Jordan River. As soon as the feet of the priests touched the water, the river stopped flowing. No water flowed toward the Dead Sea. The priests stood in the middle of the dry riverbed near Jericho while everyone else crossed over.

They marched quickly past the sacred chest and into the desert near Jericho. As soon as the priests carried the chest past the highest place that the floodwaters of the Jordan had reached, the river flooded its banks again. That's how the Lord showed the Israelites that Joshua was their leader. For the rest of Joshua's life, the people respected him as they had respected Moses.

The People Set Up a Monument

Joshua 4:1-9

After Israel had crossed the Jordan, the Lord said to Joshua, "Tell one man from each of the twelve tribes to pick up a large rock from where the priests are standing. Then have the men set up those rocks as a monument at the place where you camp tonight."

Joshua chose twelve men. He called them together and told them, "Go to the middle of the riverbed where the sacred chest is, and pick up a large rock. Carry it on your shoulder to our camp. There are twelve of you, so there will be one rock for each tribe.

Someday your children will ask, 'Why are these rocks here?' Then you can tell them how the water stopped flowing when the chest was being carried across the river. These rocks will always remind our people of what happened here today."

The men followed the instructions that the Lord had given Joshua. They picked up twelve rocks, one for each tribe, and carried them to the camp.

Joshua had some other men set up a monument next to the place where the priests were standing. This monument was also made of twelve large rocks. It is still there in the middle of the river.

The Battle of Jericho

Joshua 6:1-14

Meanwhile, the people of Jericho had been locking the gates in their town. They were afraid of the Israelites. No one could go out or come in.

The Lord said to Joshua, "With my help, you and your army will defeat the king of Jericho and his army. Here is how to do it:

March slowly around Jericho once a day for six days. Take along the sacred chest and have seven priests walk in front of it, carrying trumpets. But on the seventh day, march slowly around the town seven times while the priests blow their trumpets. Then the priests will blast on their trumpets, and everyone else will shout. The

wall will fall down, and your soldiers can go straight in from every side."

Joshua called the priests together and said, "Take the chest and have seven priests carry trumpets and march ahead of it."

Next Joshua ordered the army, "March slowly around Jericho. Don't shout the battle cry until the day I tell you to. Then let out a shout!"

Early the next morning, the seven priests blew their trumpets while everyone marched slowly around Jericho. Then they returned to camp. They did this once a day for six days.

The Walls
Come Tumbling Down

Joshua 6: 15-27

On the seventh day, the army got up at daybreak. They went around Jericho seven times. Then the priests blew the trumpets.

Joshua yelled, "Get ready to shout! The Lord will let you capture this town. Show that it now belongs to the Lord! The woman Rahab helped the spies we sent, so protect her and the others who are inside her house. But kill everyone else in the town. The silver and gold and everything made of bronze and iron belong to the Lord and must be put in his treasury."

The priests blew their trumpets again, and the soldiers shouted as loud as they could. The walls of Jericho fell flat. Then the soldiers rushed up the hill, went straight into the town, and captured it.

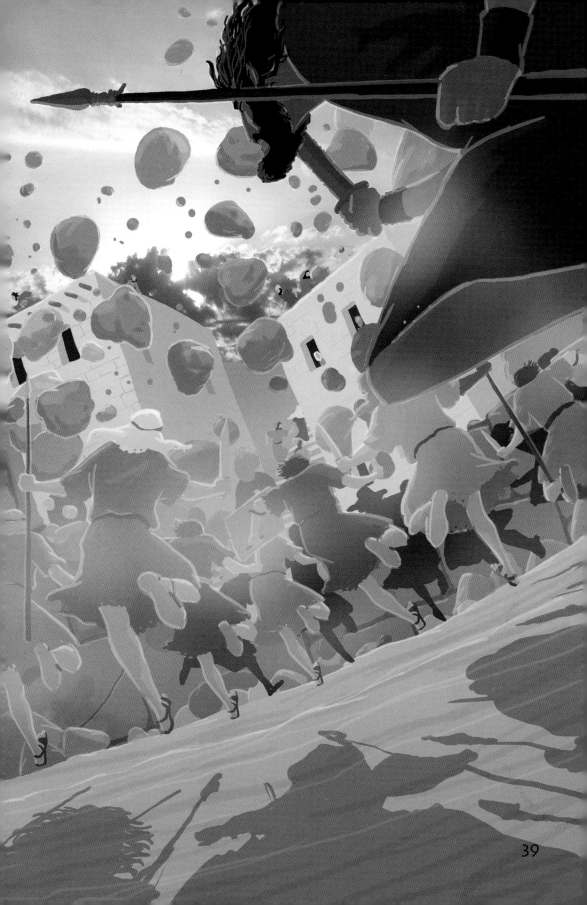

Joshua Commands the Sun to Stand Still

Joshua 10:1-15

Five Amorite kings called their armies together and attacked Gibeon. The Gibeonites sent a message to the Israelite camp saying, "Joshua, please come and rescue us! The Amorite kings from the hill country have joined together and are attacking us. We are your servants, so don't let us down. Please hurry!"

Joshua and his army left their camp. "Joshua," the Lord said, "Don't be afraid of the Amorites. They will run away when you attack, and I will help you defeat them."

Joshua marched all night to Gibeon and made a surprise attack on the Amorite camp.

The Lord made the enemy panic, and the Israelites started killing them right and left. They chased the Amorite troops up the road. The Lord made huge hailstones fall on them. More of the enemy soldiers died from the hail than from the Israelite weapons.

About noon, Joshua prayed to the Lord, "Our Lord, make the sun stop in the sky over Gibeon."

The sun stood still and didn't go down for about a whole day until Israel defeated its enemies. Never before and never since has the Lord done anything like that for someone who prayed. The Lord was really fighting for Israel. After the battle, Joshua and the Israelites went back to their camp.

"We Will Worship and Obey the Lord"

Joshua 24:14-28

Then Joshua told the people, "Worship the Lord, obey him, and always be faithful. Will you worship the same idols your ancestors did? Or since you're living on land that once belonged to the Amorites, maybe you'll worship their gods. I won't. My family and I are going to worship and obey the Lord!

The people answered, "The Lord is our God. We were slaves in Egypt, but we saw the Lord work miracles to set our people free. Even though other nations were all around us, the Lord protected us wherever we went. And when we fought the Amorites and the other nations that lived in this land, the Lord made them run away."

Joshua said, "But you still have some idols. Get rid of your idols! You must decide once and for all that you really want to obey the Lord God of Israel."

The people said, "The Lord is our God, and we will worship and obey only him."

Joshua made laws for Israel and wrote them down in The Book of the Law of God. Then he set up a large stone under the oak tree at the place of worship in Shechem.

He told the people, "Look at this stone. It has heard everything that the Lord has said to us. Our God can call this stone as a witness if we ever reject him."

Then Joshua sent everyone back to their homes.

Israel in the Promised Land

Joshua 21: 43-45

The Lord gave the Israelites the land he had promised their ancestors. They captured it and settled in it. There still were enemies around Israel, but the Lord kept his promise to let his people live in peace. And whenever the Israelites did have to go to war, no enemy could defeat them. The Lord always helped Israel win. The Lord promised to do many good things for Israel, and he kept his promise every time.

Joshua's Farewell Speech

Joshua 23: 1-14

The Lord let Israel live in peace with its neighbors for a long time. Joshua lived to a ripe old age. One day he called a meeting of the leaders of the tribes of Israel.

He told them, "I am now very old. You have seen how the Lord your God fought for you and helped you defeat the nations who lived in this land. There are still some nations left, but the Lord has promised you their land. So when you attack them, he will make them run away."

"Be sure that you carefully obey everything written in The Book of the Law of Moses and do

exactly what it says. Don't have anything to do with the nations that live around you. Don't worship their gods or pray to their idols. Be as faithful to the Lord as you have always been."

"Any one of you can defeat a thousand enemy soldiers because the Lord God fights for you. Be sure to always love the Lord your God. Don't ever turn your backs on him. I will soon die, as everyone must. But deep in your hearts you know that the Lord has kept every promise he ever made to you. Not one of them has been broken."

Judah's Army Defeats the Enemies

Judges 1:1-15

After the death of Joshua, the Israelites asked the Lord, "Which of our tribes should attack the Canaanites first?"

"Judah!" the Lord answered. "I'll help them take the land."

Judah's army fought the Canaanites, and the Lord helped Judah defeat them. Judah's army went to attack Kiriath-Sepher. Caleb told his troops, "The man who captures Kiriath-Sepher can marry my daughter Achsah."

Caleb's nephew Othniel captured the town, so Caleb let

him marry Achsah.

Right after the wedding, Achsah started telling Othniel that he ought to ask her father for a field. She went to see her father. While she was getting down from her donkey, Caleb asked, "What's bothering you?"

She answered, "I need your help. The land you gave me is in the Southern Desert. Please give me some spring-fed ponds for a water supply."

Caleb gave her a couple of small ponds named Higher Pond and Lower Pond.

The Lord Chooses Leaders for Israel

Judges 2:16-19

From time to time, the Lord would choose special leaders known as judges. These judges would lead the Israelites into battle and defeat the enemies that made raids on them. In years gone by, the Israelites had been faithful to the Lord. Now they were quick to be unfaithful. They often refused even to listen to these judges. Instead of worshiping the Lord, the Israelites would worship other gods.

When enemies made life miserable for the Israelites, the Lord would feel sorry for them. He would choose a judge and help that judge rescue Israel from its enemies. The Lord would be kind to Israel as long as that judge lived. But afterwards, the Israelites would become even more sinful than their ancestors had been. The Israelites were stubborn—they simply would not stop worshiping other gods or following the teachings of other religions.

Rescued by Othniel

Judges 3:7-11

The Israelites sinned against the Lord by forgetting him and worshiping idols of Baal and Astarte. This made the Lord angry, so he let Israel be defeated by King Cushan Rishathaim of northern Syria. He ruled Israel eight years and made everyone pay taxes.

The Israelites begged the Lord for help. The Lord chose Othniel to rescue them.

The Spirit of the Lord took control of Othniel, and he led Israel in a war against Cushan Rishathaim. The Lord gave Othniel victory. Israel was at peace until Othniel died about forty years later.

God Chooses Ehud

Judges 3:12-20

Once more the Israelites started disobeying the Lord. So the Lord let them be defeated by King Eglon of Moab. Eglon and his army captured Jericho. Then he ruled Israel for eighteen years and forced the Israelites to pay heavy taxes. The Israelites begged the Lord for help. The Lord chose Ehud from the Benjamin tribe to rescue them.

They put Ehud in charge of taking the taxes to King Eglon. But before Ehud went, he made a double-edged dagger. Ehud strapped the dagger to his right thigh, where it would be hidden under his robes.

Ehud and some other Israelites took the taxes to King Eglon, who was a very fat man. As soon as they gave the taxes to Eglon, Ehud said it was time to go home. Ehud went with the

other Israelites as far as Gilgal.
Then he turned and went back.
Ehud went upstairs to the room
where Eglon had his throne.
Ehud said, "Your Majesty, I need
to talk with you in private. I have
a message for you from God!"
The king's officials left the room.
Eglon stood up as Ehud came
closer.

Ehud Kills the King

Judges 3:21-30

Ehud pulled out the dagger and shoved it so far into Eglon's stomach that even the handle was buried in his fat. Ehud left the dagger there. Then he climbed through a window onto the porch and left.

The king's officials came back and saw that the doors were locked. They said, "The king is probably inside relieving himself." They stood there waiting, but Eglon never opened the doors. Finally, they unlocked the doors, and found King Eglon lying dead on the floor.

Ehud had already escaped to the town of Seirah in the hill country and started blowing a signal on a trumpet. The Israelites came together, and he shouted, "Follow me! The Lord will help us defeat the Moabites."

The Israelites followed Ehud down to the Jordan valley. They captured the places where people cross the river on the way to Moab and killed ten thousand Moabite warriors.

Moab was so badly defeated that it was a long time before they were strong enough to attach Israel again. And Israel was at peace for eighty years.

58

Deborah and Barak

Judges 4:1-16, Judges 4:23

After the death of Ehud, the Israelites again started disobeying the Lord. So the Lord let the Canaanite king conquer Israel. For twenty years life was miserable for the Israelites. They begged the Lord for help.

Deborah was a prophet and a leader of Israel during those days. She would sit under Deborah's Palm Tree where Israelites would come and ask her to settle their legal cases.

One day, Deborah sent word for Barak to come and talk with her. When he arrived, she said, "You are to get together an army of ten thousand men and lead them to Mount Tabor. The Lord will trick Sisera and his army into coming out to fight. They will have their chariots, but the Lord has promised to help you defeat them."

"I'm not going unless you go!" Barak told her.

"All right, I'll go!" she replied. "But I'm warning you that the Lord is going to let a woman defeat Sisera. No one will honor you for winning the battle."

Then Deborah and Barak left.

The Lord Fights for Israel

Judges 4:10-24

Barak called together the ten thousand soldiers. Deborah went too.

Sisera learned that Barak had led an army to Mount Tabor. He called his troops together and got all nine hundred iron chariots ready. Then he led his army to the Kishon River.

Deborah shouted, "Barak, it's time to attack Sisera! Because today the Lord is going to help you defeat him. In fact, the Lord has already gone on ahead to fight for you."

Barak led his ten thousand troops down from Mount Tabor.

During the battle, the Lord confused Sisera, his chariot drivers, and his whole army. Everyone was so afraid of Barak and his army that even Sisera jumped down from his chariot and tried to escape.

Barak's forces went after Sisera's chariots, and Sisera's entire army was wiped out.

That day the Israelites defeated the Canaanite king, and his army was no longer powerful enough to attack the Israelites.